Gluten-Free Chinese Home Cooking

Cheryl Tidwell

D1738807

Contents

Introduction

Home-cooked Chinese dishes are so different than the Chinese food we can get in the restaurants here in America. The dishes won't have that heavy tasting, oily texture that you will often get in a Chinese restaurant. This book shows you how to make healthier Chinese food that tastes good. This "Gluten Free Chinese Home Cooking" cook book has 3 parts, including the Main Courses, Side Dishes and Fried Rice and Noodles, for a total of 43 popular Chinese home cooking recipes.

All of the ingredients, sauces and seasonings used below are GLUTEN FREE and almost all of them can be found in the regular grocery stores.

And if you don't have to eat gluten free food, you can still cook all the recipes – just switch the sauces and seasonings to your favorite brands. Just be aware that many of the gluten-free sauces aren't as salty as the regular sauces, so just adjust to taste.

I recommend that for families of four or five, you cook one dish from the Main Courses section and two or three dishes from the Side Dishes section to eat with your favorite kind of rice.

Cook the rice according to the instructions. Since all the food already has a lot of flavor, there is no need to put any butter or more seasoning in the rice. If you like to eat rice a lot, I would really recommend getting a rice cooker; it will be so much easier, and some rice cookers can be used as a steamer too.

I hope you enjoy the food!

Before you start cooking.......

In this book, for easy measurement and to avoid confusion, I would use measuring cups and measuring spoons to measure all the ingredients.

1 cup = 240 ml

1 tablespoon= 1 T = 15 ml

1 teaspoon = 1 t = 5 ml

1 tablespoon = 3 teaspoons

The sauces and the seasonings used in this book:

- San-J Tamari Gluten-Free Soy Sauce
- Kikkoman Gluten-Free Soy Sauce

- Chinese Five Spice Powder
- Sesame Oil
- Rice Vinegar
- Gluten-Free Oyster Sauce
- Kikkoman Gluten-Free Soy Sauce
- Cooking MiChiu (Rice Wine)

- Sweet Potato Starch
- Corn Starch
- Potato Starch

Note: Some of the amounts of food shown in the ingredient pictures are not the total amount for cooking the dish; the pictures are just to show how the ingredients are supposed to look. Please follow the recipes.

Main Course Dishes

Baked Chicken

4-5 servings

Ingredients

- 8 boneless skinless chicken thighs

Marinade

- Half an apple
- 4 cloves of garlic (skin off)
- 4 green onions
- ¾ cup of soy sauce
- 5 tablespoons of sugar
- 2 tablespoons of sesame oil
- 2 tablespoons of rice wine
- ¼ teaspoon of black pepper

Preparation

1. Wash the apple and garlic and then put all the ingredients for the marinade in the blender; blend well.
2. Put the chicken thigh in a gallon bag and add the marinade to the bag.
3. Put it in the fridge to marinate for four hours.
4. Massage the chicken and turn them over while in the fridge.
5. Preheat oven to 400 degrees.
6. Remove the chicken from the marinade. Bake the chicken, skin side down, for twenty minutes.
7. Brush both sides of the chicken with the marinade and turn over.
8. Continue baking for another fifteen minutes and enjoy.

Deep Fried Pork Chop

4-5 servings

Ingredients
- 8 boneless thin cut pork chops (about 4 oz each)
- 2 eggs beaten
- 1 ½ cups oil
- 1 cup sweet potato starch (or I cup of corn starch and 2 cups original corn flakes)

Marinade
- 2/3 cup soy sauce
- 2 cloves of garlic diced
- ½ teaspoon garlic powder
- ¼ teaspoon black pepper
- ¼ teaspoon ground cinnamon powder
- 1 tablespoon sugar
- 1 tablespoon rice wine

Preparation

1. Mix all the ingredients for the marinade in a gallon bag.
2. Put the pork in to marinate for 4 hours, massage the meat and turn them over a couple times.
3. Take the pork chops out; gently shake off the juice.
4. Dip the pork chops in the egg then coat it with the sweet potato starch; pack it tightly. Set aside for a few minutes.
5. Use medium-high heat to deep fry the pork chop until both sides are golden brown and the meat is cooked through.
6. Take the pork chops out, use a paper towel to soak off the extra oil and then sprinkle a little bit of black pepper and enjoy.

Tips

1. If you can't find sweet potato starch, dip the pork chops in the egg, then corn starch, then dip the pork chops in the eggs again. Then coat it lightly with 2 cups of original corn flakes (put them in the storage bag and crush them to fine pieces).
2. Turn the heat to high heat right before taking out the meat; that way it will help the meat to not be as greasy.
3. You can also pan fry the pork chops without any breading.
4. If you can't find rice wine, white cooking wine should work, too, or you could cook it without using any wine.

Three Sauce Chicken

4-5 servings

Ingredients

- 8 drumsticks
- 4-5 slices of ginger
- 5-6 garlic cloves with the skin off
- 1-2 sprigs of fresh basil leaves
- 2/3 cup of soy sauce
- 2/3 cup of rice wine
- 1/4 cup of sesame oil
- 1 tablespoon of sugar

Preparation

1. Cut the drumsticks in half, and wipe off the moisture.
2. Turn on the high heat to heat ¼ cup of sesame oil in the wok until the oil is hot.
3. Add the ginger and stir fry them until it looks kind of dry.
4. Add the chicken and stir fry for about five minutes.
5. Add 1 tablespoon of sugar, stir well.
6. Add 2/3 cup soy sauce and stir well. Make sure each piece of chicken is well-coated with the sauce.
7. Then add 2/3 cup of rice wine, cooking until it boils.
8. Continue cooking for 2-3 minutes.
9. Turn to medium-low heat and put the garlic in.
10. Continue cooking for 30 minutes without the lid.
11. Stir every few minutes and make sure that the chicken is cooked all the way through in the sauce and not burned.
12. Add the basil in and continue cooking for 30 more minutes. Enjoy.

Tips

1. Put the drumsticks in the freezer for about 3 hours then cut the drumsticks into half with the meat saw. It will be easier and have a clean cut on the chicken.
2. If you don't like the bottom part of the drumstick you can use the small piece of bone-in thigh.

3. Basil is very important for this dish. I prefer to use Thai basil, but if you can't find Thai basil any other basil is fine, too.
4. The sauce is great to put on top of the rice to eat.
5. Be careful: it might have small pieces of bone in the sauce.

Green Onion Stew Beef

4-5 servings

Ingredients

- 2½ pounds of beef, cut into big chunks
- 4 green onions cut into strips
- 4-5 slices of ginger
- 1 cup of soy sauce
- 2 tablespoons sugar
- 2 cups of water
- 2 tablespoons oil

Preparation

1. Put beef in a pot of cold water over the meat, turn the heat on the "lowest setting." Cook the beef in the water for 30 minutes. Wash and drain the water.
2. Use high heat to heat 2 tablespoons oil.
3. Add the green onion, the white part in first, and stir for a few seconds. Add ginger, and stir well.
4. Add beef and the rest of the green onion, stir everything well, and cook for a couple minutes.
5. Add 2 tablespoons sugar, stir, add 1 cup of soy sauce, and stir again.
6. Add ½ cup of rice wine. Stir for a few seconds, then add 2 cups of water. Bring to a boil and cook for a couple minutes.
7. Turn the heat down to low, cover with the lid, and continue cooking for 3 hours until the beef is tender.

Tips

1. I would recommend using the shank or chuck roast parts to cook this dish, so it won't be too dry.

2. The beef shank we can find in the grocery store is usually like shank steak with a bone in the center; just put it in the freezer for a couple hours and then cut the meat off the bone into big pieces.
3. Beef contains a lot of water, cut the beef in big chunks so it won't shrink too much after cooking.

Pineapple Shrimp

4-5 servings

Ingredients

- 1 pound of raw shrimp
- 1 cup of canned pineapple chunks
- 2 tablespoons corn starch
- 1 egg white
- 1 cup of potato starch
- 1 teaspoon salt
- 2 cups of oil

Sauce

- 5 tablespoons mayonnaise
- 2 tablespoons sugar
- 2 tablespoons pineapple juice from the can

Preparations:

1. Remove the shells from the shrimp, wash and drain the water.
2. Use ½ teaspoon salt, 1 egg white and 2 tablespoons corn starch to marinate the shrimp for 10 minutes.
3. Mix the ingredients of the sauce together first; set aside.
4. Bread the shrimp with 1 cup of potato starch.
5. Heat 2 cups of oil; when the oil is hot put the shrimp in to deep fry until the shrimp is half way done. Take the shrimp out and set aside.
6. After a few seconds put shrimp back in to refry them again for 5 seconds.
7. Turn the heat on high before taking the shrimp out. Put the shrimp on the paper towel to soak off the extra oil.
8. Turn the heat off, dump the oil out of the wok or pot, and use paper towels to gently wipe off the leftover oil in the wok.
9. Dump the premixed sauce from above into the wok. Stir for a few seconds, add shrimp back in. The electric stove should still be hot; use the heat to mix the shrimp and sauce well. Add pineapple, stir well and serve.

Tips

- If you can't find potato starch just use corn starch instead.

- If you have a gas stove, on the last step turn on the lowest heat to finish mixing everything.

Soy Sauce Stew Ground Pork

4-5 servings

Ingredients

- 1 pound of ground pork
- 4 dry or fresh shiitake mushrooms minced
- 1 big shallot minced
- 4-5 boiled eggs with the shells off
- ¼ cup of soy sauce + 2 teaspoons of salt
- 1 tablespoon of oil
- ½ tablespoon of brown sugar
- ¼ cup of rice wine
- ¼ teaspoon of Chinese 5 spice

Preparation
1. Use high heat to heat 1 tablespoon of oil.

2. When the oil is hot, add the shallots to cook for a few minutes until the good smell comes out and until the shallots look kind of dry.
3. Add the mushrooms to cook for a few minutes.
4. Add the ground pork and stir well; then turn the heat down to medium low to cook the pork for 20 minutes. Only stir a couple times.
5. Turn the heat back up high and add ½ tablespoon of sugar and a ¼ cup of soy sauce and the Chinese 5 spice and stir them. Add 2 teaspoons of salt.
6. Add ¼ cup of rice wine and stir again, and then add 2 ½ cups of water and stir well. Bring to a boil for a couple minutes.
7. Add the eggs in and cook to a boil again.
8. Turn the heat down to low and cover with the lid and continue cooking for an hour.
9. Serve on noodles (like meat sauce on spaghetti noodles) or rice.

Tips

- Fresh shiitake mushroom can be found in regular grocery stores, the dried ones can be found in Sprouts or other health food stores.
- If you use the dry mushrooms, they need to be soaked in water to soften them before you use them.
- This dish goes really well with the cooked napa cabbage and rice.

Pan Fried Fish

4-5 servings

Ingredients

- 5 tilapia or white fish fillets
- Lawry's seasoning salt
- Onion powder
- Black pepper
- 1 tablespoon oil

Preparation

1. Rinse the fish and wipe off the water.
2. Use medium heat to heat 1 tablespoon oil.
3. When the oil is hot put the fish fillets in to cook until both sides are golden brown.
4. Sprinkle Lawry's seasoning salt, onion powder and black pepper to taste.

Tips

- If you use frozen fish, the fish will need to be thawed out first; make sure to wipe off any extra moisture.
- When cooking the fish, it is really easy for the fish to stick to the pan. Make sure there is enough oil and it's hot enough before putting the fish in.
- Don't keep turning it over, cook one side until it's done and seasoned and then turn to the other side to cook.

Boiled Chicken

4-5 servings

Ingredients

- 8 pieces of chicken (4 legs and 4 thighs)

Dipping sauce

- 2 green onions minced
- 20 grams of ginger minced
- 3 tablespoons soy sauce
- 1 tablespoon sesame oil
- 1 tablespoon sugar
- 5 tablespoons water

Preparation

1. Boil a big pot of water with enough water to cover the chicken.
2. Put the chicken in; bring it to a boil.
3. Use high heat to cook chicken for 5 minutes.
4. Turn the heat off; cover with the lid and let the chicken simmer for 5 minutes.
5. Repeat steps 3 and 4 two more times.
6. After the chicken has finished simmering for the third time, turn the heat on high to bring it to a boil again, then turn the heat off right away.
7. Take the chicken out and soak it in ice water for 5 minutes.
8. Heat 1 tablespoon sesame oil, add minced green onions and ginger. Stir well, and add soy sauce and sugar. Bring to a boil for dipping sauce.
9. Serve it with the dipping sauce.

Tips

- Use a strainer to strain the water that was used to cook the chicken; that can then be used for the chicken broth.

Pork Ribs with Salt and Pepper

4-5 servings

Ingredients

- 1 ½ pounds pork rib tips
- 2 green onions minced
- 3 cloves of garlic minced
- 1 egg beaten
- 1 ½ cups potato starch (or corn starch)
- ½ teaspoon salt
- ¼ teaspoon pepper
- 2 cups of oil

Marinade

- 2 tablespoons soy sauce
- 1 tablespoon rice wine
- 2 teaspoons sugar
- ¼ teaspoon garlic powder

Preparation

1. Cut the pork ribs into small pieces and trim the extra fat off.
2. Put the ribs in a pot of cold water. Cover the ribs and cook with the very lowest heat for 30 minutes. (The purpose of this step is to get rid of the gamey taste, so it's more about soaking the meat, rather than cooking it.)
3. Wash and drain the water off. Marinate the ribs with 2 tablespoons soy sauce, 1 tablespoon rice wine, 2 teaspoons sugar and ¼ teaspoon garlic powder for 10 minutes.
4. Mix well ½ teaspoon of salt and ¼ teaspoon of pepper first, set aside.
5. Gently shake the extra sauce off the ribs, dip the ribs in the egg and then coat it lightly with potato starch. Set aside.
6. Heat 2 cups of oil; deep fry the pork ribs until they are about 70% cooked. Take them out and set aside for a couple minutes.
7. Turn the heat on high and put the ribs back in to deep fry again, until the ribs are cooked through and golden brown.
8. Take them out and set them on paper towels to soak off the extra oil.
9. Dump the oil out and use paper towels to wipe off the leftover oil in the wok.
10. Turn the heat on high, add green onion and garlic and stir for a couple minutes.

11. Add ribs in, sprinkle the salt and pepper mix, then stir well for another couple minutes and enjoy.

Tips

- If you can't find rice wine just use water instead.

Onion Beef

4-5 servings

Ingredients

- 300 grams of thin sliced beef
- 1 small onion
- 8 ounces of mushrooms
- 1 clove of garlic minced
- 2 green onions minced
- 1 ½ tablespoon soy sauce + 1 teaspoon salt
- 1 ½ tablespoon oyster sauce
- 1 teaspoon oil
- 1 cup of water
- Pepper
- Corn starch water: 1 tablespoon corn starch + 4 tablespoons water

Preparation

1. Cut the beef and mushrooms into small slices.
2. Cut the onion into strips.
3. Use high heat to heat 1 teaspoon oil.
4. Add green onion to cook for a few seconds, then add garlic and stir.
5. Add onion and stir for a few seconds.
6. Add beef slices in and stir everything well for a couple minutes. Add mushrooms and stir again.
7. Add 1 ½ tablespoon soy sauce, 1 ½ tablespoon oyster sauce, 1 teaspoon salt and a dash of pepper, stir well.
8. Add 1 cup of water and bring to a boil.
9. Turn heat down to medium low, continue cooking for 5 minutes.
10. Turn heat back up high, add corn starch water, bring to a boil again and stir well, then serve with rice.

Tips

- If you use bigger pieces of meat, you should marinate the beef with a little soy sauce, pepper and corn starch for few minutes, use some oil to cook the beef first, then set aside. Then continue following the recipe.

Deep Fried Chicken Strips

4-5 servings

Ingredients

- 2 pounds of chicken breast or thigh cut into strips
- 2 cups of sweet potato flour
- 1 egg beaten
- 2 cups of oil

Marinade

- 4 cloves of garlic minced
- 1 teaspoon garlic powder
- 6 tablespoons soy sauce
- 3 tablespoons sugar
- ½ teaspoon black pepper
- 2 tablespoons rice wine
- 1/8 teaspoon Chinese 5 spices

Preparation

- In a gallon bag put 4 cloves of minced garlic, 1 teaspoon garlic powder, 6 tablespoons soy sauce, 3 tablespoons sugar, ½ teaspoon black pepper, 2 tablespoons rice wine and 1/8 teaspoon Chinese 5 spices. Marinate the chicken for 4 hours.
- Gently shake off the extra sauce, dip the chicken strips in the egg, then coat it with the sweet potato flour; set aside for a couple minutes.
- Heat 2 cups of oil, then deep fry the chicken strips until the chicken is cooked through and golden brown.
- Turn heat back on high before taking the chicken out. Put the chicken strips on the paper towel to absorb the extra oil.
- Sprinkle with a little black pepper and enjoy.

Tips

1. If you can't find sweet potato flour just use corn starch instead.
2. If you can't find rice wine you can use water instead.
3. Chinese 5 spices can be found in regular grocery stores.

Side Dishes

Corn and Pork Stir Fry

4-5 servings

Ingredients

- 2 fresh corn cobs
- 4 ounces of pork cut into small strips (you can also use chicken)
- 2 green onions minced
- 2 cups of water
- 1 teaspoon of oil
- Corn starch water: 1 tablespoon of corn starch + 3 tablespoons of water, mixed well

Preparation

1. Cut the corn off the cob and then wash and drain the water.
2. Heat 1 teaspoon of oil in the wok, cook the green onion and then add the pork strips.
3. Cook until the pork starts to change color.
4. Add the corn in and stir everything well.
5. Add two cups of water and bring to a boil.
6. Cover the wok with the lid and cook with medium heat for five more minutes.
7. Turn the heat to high and add the corn starch water mixture; bring to a boil.
8. Salt and pepper to taste, stir well and serve.

Two Pepper with Pork

4-5 servings

Ingredients

- 12 ounces of pork strips
- Half a green pepper
- Half a red pepper
- 3 tablespoons oil + 1 teaspoon oil
- Corn starch water: 1 tablespoon of corn starch + 5 tablespoons of water, mixed well

Marinade

- 1 ½ tablespoon of rice wine
- 1 ½ tablespoon of soy sauce
- ½ tablespoon of sugar
- 1 tablespoon of corn starch

Seasoning

- 1 ½ teaspoon of salt
- 1 ½ tablespoon of soy sauce

- 4 tablespoons of water

Preparation

1. Marinade the pork strips with the marinade for 10 minutes. Before cooking, add 1 tablespoon of corn starch to the pork and mix well.
2. Cut the green pepper and red pepper into strips and then soak them in hot water for three minutes; drain the water out well.
3. Heat 3 tablespoons of oil and cook the pork strips until it is about 70% cooked.
4. Put the pork into a strainer to drain out the extra oil and then set aside.
5. Using high heat, heat 1 teaspoon of oil and add the peppers, stir well.
6. Add the pork back in and then cook until the pork is completely done.
7. Add all the seasonings, stir well, then add the corn starch water. Bring to a boil and serve.

Tips

- For the hot water used to soak the peppers, just use the hottest tap water .

Stir Fry Potato

4-5 servings

Ingredients

- 2 medium potatoes
- 3 green onions minced
- 1 teaspoon white vinegar
- 1 teaspoon oil
- 1 cup of water
- Salt
- Pepper

Preparation

1. Peel the potatoes. Cut the potatoes into thin slices and then cut them to long strips.
2. Wash potato strips with cold water and rinse; repeat 3 times.
3. Soak potato strips in cold water in a straining bowl. Add 1 teaspoon vinegar and soak for 30 minutes. Drain and rinse the potatos.
4. Use high heat to heat 1 teaspoon oil, cook green onion for a few seconds, add potatoes and stir well.
5. Add 1 cup water and turn the heat down to medium heat.
6. Cook potato until the potatoes start to turn transparent, then continue cooking for a couple more minutes.
7. Add salt and pepper to taste.

Stir Fry Edamame with Pork

4-5 servings

Ingredients

- 8 ounces of frozen shelled edamame beans
- 4 ounces of pork cut into small strips (you can also use chicken)
- 1 clove of garlic, diced
- ½ teaspoon of oil
- 1 teaspoon of soy sauce
- 2/3 cup of water
- Salt and pepper

Preparation

1. Wash the frozen edamame beans and drain the water out. (You don't need to thaw them.)
2. Use the 1 teaspoon of soy sauce and a dash of pepper to marinate the pork strips for 3 minutes.
3. Heat the 1 teaspoon of oil, add garlic and cook for a few seconds.
4. Add the pork strips and cook until the pork is halfway cooked.
5. Add the edamame and stir everything together.
6. Add 2/3 cup of water and bring it to a boil.
7. Turn the heat to medium heat.
8. Continue cooking for two to three minutes.
9. Add salt and pepper to taste.

Bamboo Shoots Cook Pork

4-5 servings

Ingredients

- 2 cans (8 ounces each) of bamboo shoots
- 200 grams (8 ounces) of pork, cut into strips
- 2 cloves of garlic, sliced
- 3 tablespoons soy sauce
- 2/3 cup of water
- 2 teaspoons of oil

Preparations:

1. Heat 2 teaspoons of oil, then add garlic in to cook for a few seconds.
2. Add pork strips in; stir well, then cook until the pork changes color – about 80% done.
3. Add bamboo shoots, mix well.
4. Add 3 Tablespoons of soy sauce, stir well.
5. Add 2/3 cup of water; bring to a boil, then taste to see if the flavor is salty enough. Continue cooking for a couple minutes and serve.

Tips

- Canned bamboo has already been cooked, so you don't need to cook it for too long or it will lose its flavor.
- Cut the pork into smaller strips so it will cook faster.

Chicken and Celery Stir Fry

4-5 serving

Ingredients

- 4 stalks of celery cut to small pieces
- 200 grams (about 8 ounces) chicken
- 1 medium carrot sliced
- 1 green onion minced
- 1 clove of garlic minced
- 1 1/2 teaspoons oil
- Corn starch water (1 tablespoon corn starch + 5 tablespoons water)
- 1 cup of water
- Salt
- Pepper

Marinade

- 2 teaspoon soy sauce
- 1 teaspoon corn starch

Preparation

1. Marinate the chicken with 2 teaspoons soy sauce, a dash of pepper, and 1 teaspoon corn starch for 10 minutes.
2. Heat 1 teaspoon oil to cook the chicken until it is halfway cooked; set aside.
3. Heat ½ teaspoon oil, add green onion cook for a few seconds, then add garlic and stir well.
4. Add the chicken and stir for a few seconds.
5. Add carrots and celery; mix well.
6. Add 1 cup of water and stir well, bring to a boil, and continue cooking for a couple minutes.
7. Add corn starch water; bring it to a boil, then salt and pepper to taste.

Pan Fry Tofu

4-5 servings

Ingredients

- 1 firm tofu (about 14 ounces)
- 2 green onions cut into strips
- 2 tablespoons soy sauce
- ½ cup of water
- 1 tablespoon oil

Preparation

1. Cut the tofu in the middle to 2 pieces from the long side, then slice them into squares, about ½" thick. Rinse with water and wipe off extra moisture.
2. With high heat, heat 1 tablespoon of oil; when the oil is hot, put the tofu in to pan fry.
3. Turn heat down to medium-low and fry the tofu until it's golden brown.
4. Turn tofu over to cook the other side.
5. At the same time put the green onion in the part of the pan that has more oil to cook with tofu.
6. Once the bottom of the tofu is golden brown, add 2 tablespoons soy sauce and ½ cup of water and then turn the heat to high; bring to a boil.
7. Then turn heat down to medium-low and cook the tofu until about half of the sauce is left. Serve.

Tips

- Don't keep stirring the tofu; cook until one side is done and then turn it over to cook on the other side.

Deep Fried Tofu

4-5 servings

Ingredients
- 1 firm tofu (about 16 oz)
- 1 cup of corn starch
- ½ teaspoon baking powder
- 2 eggs beaten
- 2 cups of oil

Sauce (mix together and set aside)
- 3 tablespoons soy sauce
- 2 tablespoons ketchup
- 2 tablespoons sugar
- 1 teaspoon vinegar
- ½ tablespoon sesame oil
- ½ tablespoon vegetable oil
- 1 tablespoon minced green onion
- 1 teaspoon minced ginger

- 1 teaspoon minced garlic
- 1 teaspoon minced cilantro

Preparation

1. Cut the tofu into 10 square pieces and rinse with water; wipe off the extra moisture.
2. Mix the corn starch with baking powder.
3. Dip the tofu in the egg.
4. Coat the tofu with the corn starch mixture.
5. Heat 2 cups of oil and put the tofu in to deep fry until golden brown on each side.
6. Serve with the sauce.

Tofu with ground pork

4-5 servings

Ingredients

- 1 soft or silken tofu (about 14 ounces) cut into 8 big pieces
- 200 grams (8 ounces) ground pork
- 1-2 green onions minced
- 1 clove garlic finely minced
- 5 tablespoons soy sauce
- Pepper
- 2 ½ cups of water
- 1 teaspoon oil
- Corn starch water: 1 tablespoon corn starch + 4 tablespoons water

Preparation

1. Heat 1 teaspoon oil, then cook the green onion and garlic for about 30 seconds.
2. Add ground pork and stir for 2-3 minutes.
3. Add 5 tablespoons soy sauce, pepper, 2 ½ cups of water, and stir well; bring to a boil.
4. Put tofu in, gently mix it with ground pork, and turn the heat down to medium-low.
5. Cover with the lid, cook for 10 minutes. Don't keep stirring it.
6. Break the tofu to smaller pieces with the spatula, continuing to cook for 10 more minutes.
7. Turn the heat back on high, add corn starch water, and bring it to a boil. Stir well and serve with rice.

Tips

- If you like spicy food, you can add a few drops of chili oil before adding the corn starch water.
- This dish usually tastes even better the next day.

Sweet and Sour Tofu

4-5 servings

Ingredients

- 1 firm or extra firm tofu (about 16 ounces)
- 2 green onion minced
- ¼ onion cut into small pieces
- ¼ green pepper cut into small pieces
- 1 tablespoon oil + 1 teaspoon oil
- Corn starch water: 1 tablespoon corn starch+ 6 tablespoons water

Sweet and sour sauce (mix first and set aside)

- 4 tablespoons soy sauce
- 3 tablespoons vinegar
- 3 tablespoons sugar
- 4 tablespoons ketchup
- ½ cup water

Preparation

1. Soak green pepper in hot water for 5 minutes.
2. Cut the tofu into small pieces.
3. Heat 1 tablespoon oil to pan fry tofu until both sides are golden brown; set aside.
4. Heat the oil, add green onion, and stir for a few seconds; then add onion, stir for a couple minutes, add green pepper, and stir everything well.
5. Gently add tofu back in, pour in the pre-mixed sweet and sour sauce, and gently mix everything well. Bring to a boil.
6. Turn the heat down to low and cook the tofu for 10 minutes.
7. Turn heat back to high, add corn starch water, and bring to a boil. Mix everything well and serve.

Tips

- Just use the hottest tap water to soak the green pepper – it doesn't have to be boiled water.
- It's easy for the tofu to stick to the pan, so make sure there is enough oil and the pan is hot before you put the tofu in.
- The sweet and sour sauce can also be used for other meat dishes like sweet and sour pork, sweet and sour chicken, etc.

Green Onion Pan Fry Eggs

4-5 servings

Ingredients

- 6 eggs beaten
- 3 green onions minced
- 1 tablespoon soy sauce
- A dash of pepper
- 1 tablespoon oil

Preparation

1. Beat the eggs, then mix the minced green onion and eggs well.
2. Add 1 tablespoon soy sauce and a dash of pepper; mix well.
3. Heat 1 tablespoon of oil; when the oil is hot pour the egg mixture in.
4. Turn the heat down to medium-low to cook the eggs.
5. When the eggs start to get hard, turn them over to cook the other side.
6. When the eggs are cooked through, cut them into small pieces and serve.

Tips

- I use a 12-inch skillet for this.

Tomato stir fry eggs

4-5 servings

Ingredients

- 1 medium red tomato
- 6 eggs, beaten
- 2 green onions, minced
- 1 teaspoon of sugar
- 2/3 cup of water
- 1 tablespoon oil + 1 teaspoon of oil
- Salt and pepper to taste

Preparation

1. Use 1 tablespoon of oil to cook the eggs in big chunks.
2. Cut the tomato into big chunks.
3. Use medium-high heat to heat up 1 teaspoon of oil and then cook the green onions.
4. Add the tomato chunks.
5. Cook them until the tomato juice starts to come out.
6. Pour the eggs and stir them, then add the sugar and stir well.
7. Add 2/3 cup of water and cook until it boils.
8. Salt and pepper to taste and enjoy!

Tips

- Roma tomatoes aren't really suitable for this dish; you need to use juicier tomatoes.

Steamed Eggs

4-5 servings

Ingredients
- 4 eggs
- 400 ml of water
- 2 tablespoons soy sauce
- ¼ teaspoon salt
- Pepper

Preparation
1. Beat 4 eggs.
2. Add 400 ml of water into the egg liquid; mix well.
3. Add 2 tablespoons soy sauce, ¼ teaspoon salt, and a dash of pepper and mix well.
4. Pour the egg moisture through a strainer with smaller holes one time.

5. In a deep pot, boil some water, then put the egg mixture in to steam on high heat for about 3 minutes. Cover up with the lid, but leave a little space open.
6. Turn the heat off, and cover with the lid to simmer for 10 minutes. Serve.

Tips

- The egg to water ratio is about 1 egg to 100 ml of water.
- You can use chicken broth instead of water.
- The more you strain the eggs through the strainer, the smoother and more tender it will make them.

Carrot Stir-Fry Eggs

4-5 servings

Ingredients

- 2 medium carrots
- 6 eggs, beaten
- 2 cloves of garlic, diced
- 1 tablespoon oil + 1 teaspoon oil
- ½ cup of water
- Salt

Preparation

1. Peel the skin off the carrots. Use a cheese grater to grate the carrots on the thicker side to make thick strips.
2. Use the 1 tablespoon of oil to cook the eggs first in big chunks; set aside.
3. Use medium heat to heat 1 teaspoon oil, add garlic, stir, add carrots strips in and stir for a few minutes.
4. Add egg chunks in and mix well.
5. Add ½ cup of water, turn the heat down to medium, continuing to cook for a couple minutes. Salt to taste.

Tips

- When cooking the eggs, don't keep stirring it so you can make the eggs in bigger chunks.

Pan-Fried Eggs with Potato

4-5 servings

Ingredients

- 1 cup shredded potato
- 7 eggs
- 2 green onions, minced
- 3 tablespoons soy sauce
- ¼ teaspoon salt
- Pepper
- 1 tablespoon oil

Preparation

1. Use the thicker side on the cheese grater to grate the potato; set aside.
2. In a big bowl mix the shredded potato, eggs and green onion together well.
3. Add 3 tablespoons soy sauce, 1/4 teaspoon salt and a dash of pepper; mix well.
4. Heat 1 tablespoon of oil. When the oil is hot, pour in the egg mixture.
5. Turn the heat down to medium-low to pan fry the eggs. Don't keep stirring them.
6. Wait until the eggs start to harden, then flip them over to cook the other side.
7. Cook the eggs until both sides are cooked through and serve.

Tips

- When cooking eggs, it's easy for them to stick to the pan; before pouring the eggs in make sure there is enough oil and the pan or wok is hot.
- I use a 12-inch skillet for this.

Pan-Fry Eggs with Shrimp

4-5 servings

Ingredients

- 200 grams (8 ounces) of raw shrimp
- 6 eggs, beaten
- 2 green onions, minced
- 2 tablespoons soy sauce
- 1 cup of water
- 1 tablespoon oil

Preparation

1. Remove the shells from the shrimp, wash and drain well, and set aside.
2. Heat 1 tablespoon of oil, then add the green onion and cook for a few seconds.
3. Add shrimp and stir for a few seconds.
4. Pour the eggs in, then turn the heat down to medium-low to cook the eggs; don't keep stirring them.
5. Once the eggs start to get hard, flip the eggs and shrimp mixture over to cook the other side.
6. Continue cooking until the eggs and shrimp are cooked through; add 2 tablespoons soy sauce, and gently stir it.
7. Add 1 cup of water and bring it to a boil and serve.

Stir-Fry Snow Peas

4-5 servings

Ingredients

- 12 ounces snow peas
- 2 cloves of garlic, diced
- ½ teaspoon of oil
- Salt and pepper

Preparation

1. Heat the wok over high heat.
2. Add ½ teaspoon of oil to the wok.
3. When the oil is hot, add the peas and stir well.
4. Add ½ a cup of water, stir and cook for 30 seconds
5. Salt to taste and serve.

Tips

- When cooking the veggies, use high heat and cook for a short time so the vegetables will stay crispy and retain their beautiful color.

Stir-Fry Green Cabbage

4-5 servings

Ingredients

- 1/8 head of green cabbage
- 1 medium-sized carrot
- 2 cloves of garlic, diced
- 2/3 cup of water
- 1 teaspoon of oil

Preparation

1. Wash the cabbage and cut into long strips, and then soak the strips in hot water for ten minutes.
2. Use a cheese grater to grate the carrot into strips using the thicker side.
3. With high heat, heat 1 teaspoon of oil, cook the garlic, add the carrots and stir well.
4. Add the cabbage in and stir well.
5. Add the water and cook until boiling.
6. When the cabbage is cooked, salt and pepper to taste.

Tips

- The hot water used to soak the cabbage doesn't have to be boiled water. Just use the hottest tap water.
- When cooking the cabbage, use high heat and cook it fast so it stays crispy and fresh.

Stir-Fry Spinach with Shrimp

4-5 servings

Ingredients

- 1 bunch of spinach
- A small handful of raw shrimp, with the shells removed
- 2 cloves of garlic, diced
- 1 teaspoon oil
- ½ cup water
- Salt to taste

Preparation
1. Wash and cut spinach in pieces.
2. Use high heat to heat 1 teaspoon oil.
3. When the oil is hot, add garlic and cook for a few seconds.
4. Add shrimp and stir, then add spinach and stir everything well.
5. Add ½ cup of water; bring to a boil.
6. Stir constantly, adding salt to taste.

Tips
- Go ahead and cook the whole bunch of the spinach. Spinach contains a lot of water, so after it's been cooked it will shrink a lot.
- When stir-frying the veggies use high heat and cook them fast.

Cooked Napa Cabbage

4-5 servings

Ingredients

- 6 leaves of napa cabbage
- 1 medium carrot
- 4 dry or fresh shiitake mushrooms
- 3 green onions, minced
- 1 ½ cups of chicken broth
- 2 tablespoons soy sauce
- 1 teaspoon oil
- Salt
- Pepper

Preparation

1. Wash the napa cabbage, then cut into big strips.
2. Peel the skin off the carrots, and cut into small slices.
3. Wash the mushrooms and cut them into small strips.
4. Heat 1 teaspoon of oil, cook the green onion for a few seconds, add mushrooms in and stir for a couple minutes.
5. Add the sliced carrots and napa cabbage, stir well, then add 2 tablespoons soy sauce.
6. Add 1 ½ cups of water and bring to a boil; cover with the lid, turn the heat down to medium low, and continue cooking for about 5 minutes until the cabbage is soft. Serve.

Tips

- Fresh shiitake mushrooms can be found in regular grocery stores, dried ones can be found in Sprouts or other health food stores.
- If you use the dry mushrooms, they need to be soaked in the water to soften them before you use them.

Stir-Fry Broccoli

4-5 servings

Ingredients

- 12 ounces of broccoli florets
- 2 cloves of garlic, diced
- ½ teaspoon of oil
- 1 cup of water
- Salt and pepper to taste

Preparation

1. Cut and wash the broccoli and drain the water.
2. Using high heat, heat the 1 teaspoon of oil.
3. Cook the garlic and add the broccoli in to cook for a couple minutes.
4. Add the cup of water and bring to a boil.
5. Salt and pepper to taste.

Stir-Fry Asparagus with Mushroom

4-5 servings

Ingredients

- 1 bunch of asparagus
- 3 large fresh shiitake mushrooms, cut into strips
- 2 baby carrots, cut into long strips
- 2 cloves of garlic, diced
- 1 teaspoon oil
- 2/3 cup of water

Preparation

1. Wash and cut the asparagus into long strips and discard the hard part.
2. Heat 1 teaspoon oil, add garlic, and stir for a few seconds.
3. Add carrots and stir; add the mushrooms and stir well.
4. Add asparagus and stir everything for a few seconds. Add 2/3 cup of water and bring to a boil.
5. Continue boiling for a couple minutes, stirring constantly until the asparagus is cooked.
6. Salt and pepper to taste.

Tips

- Fresh shiitake mushrooms can be found in regular grocery stores, dried one can be found in Sprouts or other health food stores.
- If you use the dried mushrooms, they need to be soaked in the water to soften them before you use them.

Stir-Fry Sugar Snap Peas

4-5 servings

Ingredients

- 8 ounces sugar snap peas
- 1 clove of garlic, diced
- 1 teaspoon oil
- 1 cup of water
- Salt and pepper to taste

Preparation

1. Pluck off and discard the string from each pea; wash and drain the water.
2. Heat 1 teaspoon oil, add garlic, and stir for a few seconds. Then add sugar snap peas and stir for about 30 seconds.
3. Add 1 cup of water, bring to a boil, and mix well.
4. Salt to taste and serve.

Fried Rice and Noodles

Basic Fried Rice

2-3 servings

Ingredients

- 4 cups of cooked rice
- 4 eggs
- 4 tablespoon soy sauce
- 1 tablespoon of oil
- Pepper

Preparation

1. In the wok or deep pan, heat 1 tablespoon of oil until it's hot.
2. Crack the eggs into the wok, stir the yolks and rock the wok back and forth and side to side to spread out the eggs evenly.
3. When the eggs start to get firm, flip them over to the other side and make them into big chunks.
4. Dump in the rice and stir well.
5. Add soy sauce and stir again.
6. Add the peppers and serve.

Tips

- With fried rice, it works great to use the leftover rice and the leftover meat (e.g., grilled pork) from meals you cooked before.

This is the very basic fried rice for when you don't have anything at home except rice and eggs and don't feel like going out to buy anything else.

Ham Fried Rice

3-4 serving

Ingredients

- 1 ½ cups cubed ham
- 4 cups of cooked rice (don't pack it too tight)
- 3 eggs, beaten
- 2 green onions, minced
- 1 cup frozen vegetables
- 1 tablespoon soy sauce
- 1 teaspoon salt
- Dash pepper
- 2 ½ teaspoons oil

Preparation

1. Use 1 teaspoon of oil to cook the eggs first, in big chunks.
2. Put 1 cup of water in the frozen vegetables, microwave for 1 minute, drain the water really well, and set aside.
3. Use water to rinse the ham; wipe off extra moisture.
4. Heat 1 ½ teaspoon of oil, then add green onion and cook for a few seconds.
5. Add frozen vegetables; stir well, then add ham, and mix everything well.
6. Add rice and eggs, stirring constantly until the rice is all loose and separated.
7. Add 1 tablespoon soy sauce and 1 teaspoon of salt; add a dash of pepper to taste.
8. Stir well and serve.

Tips

- Easter leftover ham is great to cook in this dish.

Baked Chicken Fried Rice

2-3 servings

Ingredients

- 2-3 baked boneless skinless chicken thighs (from the dish in the main courses section)
- 3 eggs, beaten
- 1 cup frozen vegetables
- 2 green onions minced
- 3 tablespoon of soy sauce
- 1 tablespoon of oil + 1 teaspoon of oil
- Pepper

Preparation

1. Cut the chicken into smaller pieces.
2. Using high heat, heat 1 teaspoon of oil and cook the eggs; set aside.
3. Put half a cup of water in the frozen vegetables and put in the microwave for 1 minute. Drain the water and set aside.
4. Heat 1 tablespoon of oil and cook the green onions.

5. Add the frozen vegetables and chicken and stir well.
6. Add the rice and stir everything well until the rice isn't sticking together. Add the eggs.
7. Add the soy sauce, stir again.
8. Add pepper and serve.

Tips

- Don't keep stirring the eggs so you end up with bigger chunks.

Shrimp Fried Rice

2-3 serving

Ingredients

- 4 cups cooked rice
- 8 ounces shrimp
- 3 eggs
- 2 green onions, minced
- ½ cup of baby lima beans
- ½ cup of frozen vegetables
- 1 tablespoon soy sauce
- 1 teaspoon salt
- Black pepper
- 2 teaspoons oil

Preparation

1. Use 1 teaspoon oil to cook the eggs first; make them into big chunks, then set aside.
2. Put the lima beans and frozen vegetables together, and add 1 cup of water. Microwave for 1 minute, and drain the water well.
3. Heat 2 teaspoons of oil. When the oil is hot, add green onions, stir well, add onions, and stir again.
4. Add frozen vegetables; mix everything together.
5. Add shrimp, then stir until the shrimp starts to change color.
6. Add rice and cooked egg pieces; stir everything well for a couple minutes.
7. Add 1 tablespoon soy sauce, 1 teaspoon salt and some black pepper to taste, and serve.

Green Pepper and Beef Fried Rice

2-3 servings

Ingredients

- 4 cups of cooked rice
- ¼ green pepper, cut into small strips
- ¼ onion, cut into small strips
- 200 grams (8 ounces) beef, cut into small strips
- 2 tablespoons soy sauce
- ¼ teaspoon salt
- 2 tablespoons of oyster sauce
- Dash of pepper
- 4 teaspoons oil

Marinade

- 2 tablespoons soy sauce
- 1 tablespoon rice wine
- 1 tablespoon corn starch
- 1 teaspoon sugar

- Dash of pepper

Preparation
1. Marinate the beef with 2 tablespoons soy sauce, 1 tablespoon rice wine, 1 teaspoon sugar, a dash of pepper and 1 tablespoon corn starch, for 10 minutes.
2. Soak the green pepper in hot water for 5 minutes.

3. Heat 1 teaspoon oil, add onion in, and stir for a couple minutes, then add the green pepper and stir well for another couple minutes. Set aside.
4. In the same wok or pan add 1 teaspoon oil to cook the beef until the beef changes color (about 80% done); set aside, and wash the wok or pan.
5. Heat 2 teaspoons oil, put onion and green pepper back in; stir for a few seconds, add beef back in, stir everything well, then add rice. Stir until rice is loose and separated.
6. Add 2 tablespoons soy sauce, ¼ teaspoon salt, 2 tablespoons oyster sauce and pepper to taste, mix everything well and serve.

Tips

- Just use the hottest tap water to soak the green pepper; it doesn't have to be boiled water.
- The oyster sauce doesn't taste like oysters, but it does give the food a special flavor.

Pineapple and Chicken Fried Rice

2-3 servings

Ingredients

- 4 cups of cooked rice
- 250 grams chicken cut into small pieces
- 1 cup of canned pineapple chunk
- 3 eggs, beaten
- 2 green onions, minced
- 1 cup of frozen vegetables
- 1 tablespoon soy sauce
- 1 teaspoon salt
- Pepper
- 4 teaspoons oil

Marinade

- 1 tablespoon soy sauce
- Dash of pepper
- Dash of garlic powder

Preparation

1. Marinate the chicken with 1 tablespoon soy sauce, a dash of pepper, and a dash of garlic powder for 10 minutes.
2. Heat 1 teaspoon oil to cook the eggs first; make them into big chunks, then set aside.
3. Heat 1 teaspoon oil and cook the chicken until it's about 80% done; set aside.
4. Put I cup of water in the frozen vegetables, microwave for 1 minute, drain the water out well, and set aside.
5. Heat 2 teaspoons oil, add the green onions, and stir for a few seconds.
6. Add the vegetables and stir for a few seconds.
7. Add the egg pieces and chicken, and mix everything well.
8. Add the rice and stir everything well until the rice is loose and separated.
9. Add the pineapple and mix well.
10. Add 1 tablespoon soy sauce, ½ teaspoon salt and some pepper to taste. Serve.

Tips

- The eggs will stick to the pan, so make sure that there is enough oil and the pan is hot before you put the eggs in.

Stir Fry Rice Noodle with Chicken

3-4 servings

Ingredients

- 1 package dry rice noodles (about 6.75 ounces)
- 250 grams of chicken, cut into strips
- 150 grams of green cabbage, cut into big strips
- 2 green onions, minced
- 1 medium carrot
- 1 shallot, minced
- 8 shiitake mushrooms, cut into strips
- 1 small stalk of celery, minced
- 4 tablespoons soy sauce + ½ teaspoon salt
- Pepper
- 1 teaspoon sugar
- 1 cup of chicken broth
- 1 tablespoon oil + 1 teaspoon oil

Preparation

1. Cut the chicken into strips. Marinate the chicken with 1 tablespoon soy sauce, a dash of pepper, and 1 teaspoon of sugar for 10 minutes.

2. Soak the rice noodles in room temperature water for 15 minutes, then drain the water out.
3. Wash and cut the green cabbage into big strips and then soak it in hot water for 5 minutes.
4. Peel the skin off the carrots; use the thicker side of a cheese grater to grate the carrots into strips.
5. Heat 1 teaspoon of oil to cook the chicken; cook it until it changes color, then set aside.
6. Heat 1 tablespoon of oil. When the oil is hot, add the green onions, stir for a few seconds, add the shallots, stir for few more seconds, add the mushrooms, and mix everything well by stirring for a couple more minutes.
7. Add carrots and green cabbage and stir well.
8. Add the chicken back in and stir everything together.
9. Add 4 tablespoons of soy sauce, ½ teaspoon salt, a little bit of black pepper and 1 cup of chicken broth. Mix well. Taste it to see how salty it is; make it a little bit saltier.
10. Add the rice noodles and stir everything together well.
11. Turn the heat down to medium-low and cover with the lid, continuing to cook for 5 more minutes.
12. Check it and stir constantly until the juice is reduced and the rice noodles are cooked through. Sprinkle the minced celery and serve.

Tips

- Use the hot water to soak the green cabbage. It doesn't have to be boiled water, just use the hottest tap water. If you have good quality green cabbage you don't need to presoak them.
- Different brands of rice noodles may take less or more time to cook; please adjust the cooking time as needed.
- Fresh shiitake mushrooms can be found in regular grocery stores; the dry ones need to be soaked in water until they are completely softened before use.

Stir Fry Mug Bean Noodle

2-3 servings

Ingredients

- 3 bundles dry mug bean noodles (see the picture below – there are three bundles included in the package shown)
- ½ pound ground pork
- 4 ounces green cabbage
- 1 medium carrot
- 1 clove garlic, minced
- 2 green onions, minced
- 4 tablespoons soy sauce + ¼ teaspoon salt
- Dash of pepper
- 1 tablespoon oil
- 1 ½ cups of water

Preparation

1. Soak the mug bean noodles in room temperature water for 30 minutes. Drain the water.
2. Grate the carrots with a cheese grater using the thicker side, then set aside.
3. Wash and cut the green cabbage into long pieces. Soak them in hot water for 5 minutes.
4. Heat 1 tablespoon of oil, cook the green onions, then add the garlic and cook for a few seconds.
5. Add the ground pork and stir well.
6. Add carrots and green cabbage; stir well.
7. Add 4 tablespoons of soy sauce and ¼ teaspoon of salt, and a dash of pepper. Stir again, then add 1 ½ cups of water. Taste it to see how salty it is; make it a little bit saltier.
8. Add the mug bean noodles, mix everything together well, and turn the heat down to low.
9. Cover with the lid and continue to cook for 3-5 minutes. Stir constantly until the juice is reduced and the noodles are cooked through. Serve.

Tips

1. The green cabbage we have here is kind of hard, so I soak it in the hot water first; if you have good quality cabbage you don't need to do that before cooking it.
2. For the hot water used to soak the cabbage, just use the hottest tap water. It doesn't have to be boiled water.

Beef noodle soup

1 serving

Ingredients

- 1 serving of rice noodles
- Green Onion Stew Beef with juice (see recipe above)
- 2 leaves of romaine lettuce
- 1 green onion, minced
- 1 ½ cups of chicken broth or beef broth
- 1 cup of stewed beef juice
- Dash of pepper

Preparation

1. Heat 1 1/2 cups of chicken or beef broth and 1 cup of juice from the green onion stew beef to a boil, put 3-4 pieces of beef (or however much you like) in the soup, then turn the heat off.
2. At the same time, boil a pot of water, then cook the rice noodles until they are done.
3. Take the noodles out and put them in a bowl.

4. With the same pot of the boiled water, put the romaine lettuce in to cook for a couple seconds, then take the lettuce out and put it on top of the noodles.
5. Pour the beef soup in the noodles, sprinkle the green onion on top, along with a dash of pepper. You can add chili sauce if you like it, and enjoy.

Tips
1. This dish uses the leftover beef stew to cook. Sometimes for home cooking we have so many leftovers, but we are tired of eating the same thing; just a little bit of change adds a different flavor to the food.
2. You can also cook the green onion stew beef to just go with noodle soup.
3. There are different kinds of rice noodles that are gluten free, just use the kind you like.

Made in the USA
Columbia, SC
08 January 2019